CONTENTS

WHAT IS WRESTLING?

What links Hollywood actors, Robin Williams and Tom Cruise, with former US presidents, Abraham Lincoln and George Washington? All were keen amateur wrestlers! Wrestling is an exciting sport. It is an epic battle of strength, skill and tactics between two competitors.

The World According To Garp *was written by John Irving who wrestled competitively from the ages of 14 to 34. The film version starred Robin Williams (right).*

"More enduringly than any other sport, wrestling teaches self-control and pride. Some have wrestled without great skill - none have wrestled without pride." – *US wrestling coach, Dan Gable.*

COMBAT SPORTS

WRESTLING

Clive Gifford

W
FRANKLIN WATTS
LONDON • SYDNEY

This edition 2012

First published in 2008 by
Franklin Watts
338 Euston Road
London NW1 3BH

Franklin Watts Australia
Level 17/207 Kent Street
Sydney NSW 2000

Series editor: Adrian Cole
Art director: Jonathan Hair
Design: Big Blu
Cover design: Peter Scoulding
Picture research: Luped Picture Research

A CIP catalogue record for this book is available from the British Library.

ISBN: 978 1 4451 0724 0

Dewey Classification: 796.812

Acknowledgements:
Alexander Hassenstein / Bongarts / Getty Images: 28; Alistair Scott / Alamy: 8; Arif Ali / AFP / Getty Images: 6; Aristide
Economopoulos / Star Ledger / Corbis: 14; Bettmann / Corbis: 29; Bob Thomas / Getty Images: 16; Caren Firouz / Reuters:
5, 23; Carolyn Kaster / AP Photo: 15; Cate Gillon / Getty Images: 10; Chris Trotman / NewSport / Corbis: 27b; Dagli Orti /
Agora Museum Athens / The Art Archive: 7; David Mdzinarishvili / Reuters: Front Cover; 12, 17t, 17b; Doug Pensinger /
Getty Images: 1, 26; Ermal Meta / AFP / Getty Images: 11; Kim Kyung Hoon / Reuters: 22; Lionel Preau / DPPI Final: 13;
Nati Harnik / AP Photo: 19; Nick Cunard / Rex Features: 18; Novamedia / Rex Features: 20, 21; Olivier Asselin / AP Photo:
9b; Tim Cuff / Alamy: 9t; Warner Bros / The Kobal Collection: 4; William R. Sallaz / NewSport / Corbis: 24; Yuri Kadobnov
/ AFP / Getty Images: 27t; Yves Herman / Reuters / Corbis: 25.
Every attempt has been made to clear copyright. Should there be any
inadvertent omission please apply to the publisher for rectification.

Printed in China

Franklin Watts is a division of Hachette Children's Books, an Hachette UK company.
www.hachette.co.uk

Please note: The Publishers strongly recommend seeking professional
advice and training before taking part in any contact sports. The Publishers
regret that they can accept no liability for any loss or injury sustained.

Strength, timing and control

Each wrestling contest between two wrestlers is called a bout. There are many different forms of wrestling, but all of them involve a wrestler using his or her strength and timing to gain control over their opponent. This involves gripping the opponent and sometimes throwing them to the floor. Points are awarded for various techniques during the bout.

South Korea's Kim Min-chul lifts Rawshan Ruzikulov of Uzbekistan.

SEVEN IN A ROW

At the age of 47, ten years before he became the first ever President of the United States, George Washington won seven wrestling bouts in a row against opponents from the Massachusetts Volunteer army!

AN ANCIENT HISTORY

Wrestling is one of the world's oldest sports. Archaeologists have discovered paintings of wrestlers from ancient Egypt and ancient Babylonia (Iraq), some dating back over 5,000 years.

Jiao li

In China, Jiao li wrestling developed thousands of years ago. It is the oldest Chinese martial art. By 200 BCE, Jiao li wrestlers were bodyguards to the Emperor of China.

Pehlwani wrestling

Ancient Pehlwani (or Pehalwan) wrestling from India is more than 2,500 years old and is still performed today. In the first half of the twentieth century, the greatest Pehlwani wrestler was Ghulum Mohammed, known as the Great Gama. He lost only a single match in over 5,000 wrestling bouts!

Pehlwani wrestling practised by Pakistani wrestlers at an akhra – a traditional wrestlers training institute – in Pakistan.

ANCIENT OLYMPICS

The ancient Greeks were keen wrestlers, and from 708 BCE wrestling was an event at the ancient Olympics. Legends were created there including Milo of Kroton, who is said to have won the adult wrestling competition an incredible five times in a row. The Romans took on the Greek style of wrestling, creating the Greco–Roman style still in use today.

"I swear it upon Zeus, an outstanding runner cannot be the equal of an average wrestler." – *Socrates, famous Greek scholar.*

WRESTLING AROUND THE WORLD

Compared to many combat sports which began in just one country, wrestling developed all over the world. Many forms are still popular in one country or in a specific region.

Schwingen

In Switzerland, Schwingen wrestling (below) is centuries old. Wrestlers wear shorts over their clothes. The two wrestlers hold onto their opponent's shorts and try to throw each other onto their backs.

Sumo

Sumo wrestling (right) is hugely popular in Japan. Professional wrestlers try to force each other out of a circular ring, called a *dohyo*. They can also win a bout by forcing their opponent to touch the ground with a part of their body other than their feet. The very greatest sumo wrestlers are given the title *Yokozuna*.

Evala

Evala wrestling (left) occurs every year amongst the Kaybé people of northern Togo and signals a boy's progress into adulthood.

Sambo

Sambo is a form of self-defence invented in Russia. As a sport for men and women, a bout lasts six minutes. Sambo wrestlers wear a tight jacket called a *kurka* and shorts called *trusi*.

FOLK WRESTLING

Some forms of wrestling are known as folk wrestling. They are thousands of years old, but are still performed at festivals and competitions today.

Glima wrestling

The Vikings brought Glima wrestling to Iceland over 800 years ago. It involves both wrestlers wearing a special leather belt which their opponent grips. The two wrestlers have to stand upright and step around each other in a circle.

Cumberland and Westmoreland wrestling

This is believed to have been brought to England by the Vikings. It begins with the wrestlers linking their fingers behind the back of their opponent. This hold must be kept throughout the bout as the wrestlers struggle to throw their opponent.

These wrestlers are trying to throw each other to the ground.

Oiled up

Yagli Güres is a traditional form of wrestling from Turkey. Wrestlers wear leather shorts called *kispet* and cover their bodies in slippery olive oil. Originally, there were no time limits and bouts could last for two days! Today, bouts are either 30 or 40 minutes long.

The oil makes it more difficult to get a good hold on your opponent.

Modern folkstyle

Wrestling boomed in US schools and colleges and is now called folkstyle or collegiate wrestling. It is similar to freestyle wrestling (see page 12) and allows the use of legs and arms to make holds. It places more importance on control than making big throws.

WRESTLING TODAY

Today, two forms of wrestling dominate international competitions – Greco-Roman and freestyle wrestling. Both are amateur sports where competitors are not paid to perform.

These wrestlers are battling it out in the Greco-Roman wrestling 66 kg final at the European Wrestling Championships.

What's the difference?

The key difference is that in Greco-Roman wrestling, wrestlers are not allowed to attack the legs of their opponents. All their moves and holds must be at waist height or above. In freestyle wrestling, competitors are allowed to use their legs to attack and defend with. They can also grip and hold an opponent's legs.

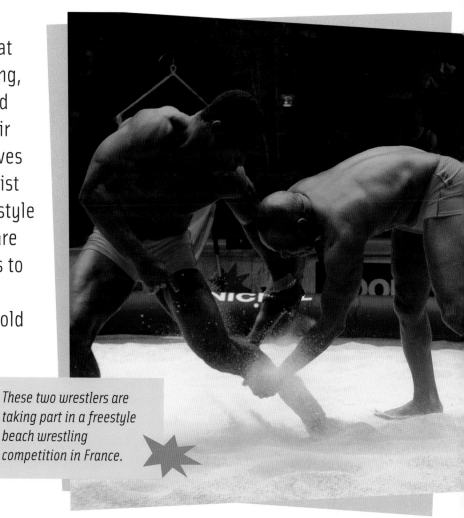

These two wrestlers are taking part in a freestyle beach wrestling competition in France.

Weight classes

In both Greco-Roman and freestyle competitions, wrestlers are divided up according to their body weight. For male Olympic wrestling there are seven weight classes: up to 55kg, 55–60kg, 60–66kg, 66–74kg, 74–84kg, 84–96kg and 96–120kg.

KEEP ON GROWING

Hungary's Gyula Bobis began wrestling in one of the lightest weight classes. As he grew in size and weight, he moved up the weight classes. By the time he wrestled at the 1948 Olympics, aged 38, he was in the heaviest class and won the gold medal!

IN TRAINING

Wrestling requires complete body fitness. Successful wrestlers of all ages train hard to improve their fitness, strength, speed of movement and their wrestling techniques.

Preparation

Wrestling involves lots of twisting and turning to avoid an opponent's attacks, as well as to make attacks. This means that parts of the body need to be stretched before training begins.

Muscles need to be stretched before training.

Mat matters

An official wrestling mat is 9 metres in diameter and is surrounded by a 1.5 metre wide border. Wrestlers always train on a mat to avoid injury.

HARD FLOOR

When South Korea's Kim Young-nam began wrestling, his school could not afford wrestling mats. He trained and practised on a hard wooden floor covered in dried rice stalks. He went on to win a gold medal at the 1988 Olympics.

Kitted out

Wrestling equipment is very simple compared to other sports. An all-in-one outfit, called a singlet, is worn in competition. It is made of stretchy material and is usually either red or blue. In training, wrestlers may wear shorts and vests. Wrestling boots are lace-up with no heels and are made of soft leather. Many junior wrestlers wear a padded headguard.

These wrestlers at Pennsylvania High School, USA, are wearing protective headgear.

"The stamina that is needed is tremendous. I cross-train with weight workouts, mountain biking, running and any way that I can move my body." – Olympic wrestler Vickie Zummo on her training programme.

TOP 10 WRESTLING MOVES 1—3

A wrestling bout begins with the two competitors trying to get a good position to attack their opponent. Tie-ups can force an opponent into a weaker position from which a headlock may be possible. The aim of these moves is to then perform a takedown – a move which brings the opponent down onto the mat.

1 Double wrist tie-up

Tie-ups are grips or holds that help wrestlers move their opponents around. The double wrist tie-up sees a wrestler grip both of his opponent's wrists firmly.

The attacking wrestler can then try to unbalance his opponent by stepping to the side or forcing his opponent's arms down.

2 Underhook

In this tie-up move a wrestler grabs under his opponent's arm and holds on to the back of his shoulder. He can control his opponent easily, or move into another hold, called a bear hug. Having two underhooks on at the same time is called a double underhook.

3 Headlock

A headlock is a hold in which an arm is wrapped around the opponent's neck and the two hands are then locked together. The opponent's arm must be inside the loop created by the attacker's hands to stop any chances of choking. From this position, the attacker may be able to make a takedown move.

MIND AND BODY

Wrestling requires mental and physical fitness. A wrestler has to be alert and determined in order to succeed. According to Olympic gold medal winner, Kendal Cross, "You really have to work hard for something that doesn't always pay off immediately."

Listening and learning

Wrestlers learn and improve their skills by working hard and listening to every word their coach says. Discipline and focus help wrestlers to compete at their best.

"You have to train the mind and the body to function and excel while someone is trying to beat you up." – *Jim Gruenwald, Olympic wrestler.*

Young wrestlers, like these, learn from their more experienced coach.

Thinking tactics

"When your head is really into a match, time seems to slow right down," says Canadian wrestler Nick Ugoalah. He won a gold medal at the 2002 Commonwealth Games and was three-times Canadian wrestling champion. Top wrestlers keep thinking throughout a bout looking for a chance to win. As Ugoalah recalls, "All through a match, I'd be probing, testing, trying to find out what made my opponent uncomfortable."

Wrestlers usually train as part of a team or a club. Respect for others in your team is also an important part of wrestling.

A WINNING MIND

Bulgarian freestyle wrestler Valentin Jordanov was famous for being incredibly strong in his mind. He had a remarkable competition record. In 685 events he won 673!

PROFESSIONAL WRESTLING

Professional wrestling bouts have occurred for hundreds of years. In the nineteenth century wrestling contests took place in circuses in the USA and Europe. Later, television brought professional wrestling to a wider audience.

Gorgeous George

George Wagner transformed professional wrestling in the 1940s and 1950s and became wrestling's first TV star. He was the first to use entrance music and wear long silk robes. He even had a butler spray his opponents with perfume before they fought!

Ring rehearsals

Modern professional wrestling features paid entertainers who rehearse their wrestling moves. Most contests take place in a roped, square ring.

Throws and moves are outrageous with action often occurring outside of the ring as well.

WRESTLING FEDERATIONS

Professional wrestling is organised by different federations, including World Wrestling Entertainment (WWE). Federations sign up wrestlers and create stories and characters for them. Feuds, grudges and outrageous acts like kidnappings occur as part of the entertainment. The top wrestlers, like The Rock, Batista and The Undertaker (below), are very famous.

RING AND REAL NAMES

Hulk Hogan - Terrence Gene Bollea
The Undertaker – Mark William Calaway
Triple H - Paul Michael Levesque
Edge – Adam Joseph Copeland
The Rock – Dwayne Johnson

TOP 10 WRESTLING MOVES 4–6

Takedowns are amongst the most exciting and most important moves in wrestling. One wrestler penetrates the other wrestler's defences and uses a range of moves or throws to bring his or her opponent down onto the mat.

4 Double leg takedown

Used in freestyle and some folk wrestling, this aggressive move sees the attacker drive her shoulder low into the attacker's stomach and grip the back of her thighs. Driving her legs forward, the wrestler tilts her opponent up and back to send her onto the mat.

5 Two-on-one to single leg takedown

Used in freestyle wrestling, this starts with the attacker gripping one of her opponent's arms with both hands and pulling it down. As the opponent tries to pull up, the attacker releases the arm and locks both her hands behind the knee of one of her opponent's legs. Keeping her back straight, she can drive up, unbalance and throw her opponent.

6 Flying Mare

This is an attacking throw used in Greco-Roman wrestling. The thrower gets his own shoulder underneath his opponent's armpit and grips his upper arm. He then drops to his knees, pulling his opponent down and over his shoulder onto the mat.

WRESTLING AT THE OLYMPICS

Wrestling has been part of the modern Olympics ever since they began in 1896. Over 100 years later, wrestling is one of the most popular Olympic sports.

Olympic action

There are Olympic competitions in both freestyle and Greco-Roman wrestling. An Olympic wrestling bout consists of six minutes of action, split into three rounds of two minutes.

Medal bouts

Wrestlers in each weight division are divided into pools. The best in each pool then go into elimination bouts until the final pair of competitors compete for the gold and silver medals.

One of the most famous bouts in Olympic history occurred in 2000. After 13 remarkable years of wrestling without losing, Russian star Aleksandr Karelin (left) finally lost a bout in the final to US wrestler, Rulon Gardner.

THE LONGEST BOUT

In the early Olympics, bouts lasted until one wrestler recorded a winning move. At the 1912 Olympics, a bout between Martin Klein and Alfred Asikainen lasted for a whopping 11 hours, 40 minutes! Klein won but was too tired to compete in the final. No wonder!

Women wrestlers

It was only in 2004 that female wrestlers were admitted into the Olympics to compete in four different weight divisions in freestyle wrestling only. The gold medallists at the 2008 games were:

Weight	Gold Medallist	Country
48 kg	Carol Huynh	Canada
55 kg	Saori Yoshida	Japan
63 kg	Kaori Icho	Japan
72 kg	Jiao Wan	China

Irini Merleni of Ukraine (red) grapples with Patricia Miranda of the USA at the 2004 Olympics. Merleni went on to win gold.

TOP 10 WRESTLING MOVES 7 — 10

Once down on the mat, both wrestlers still compete. They look for an opening or a hold or move that will win points and finish the bout. The ultimate aim is to hold an opponent's shoulders to the mat at the same time. This is a fall or pin and wins the bout.

7 Bridging

Bridging happens when a wrestler arches his or her back to keep it off the mat. Bridging is usually a defensive move to stop being pinned down, but it is also used in attack as part of the gut wrench move.

8 Gut wrench

One of the most common scoring moves on the mat, the gut wrench sees a wrestler form a strong lock of his hands around his opponent's body. He then tries to get into the bridge position and turn his opponent onto their back.

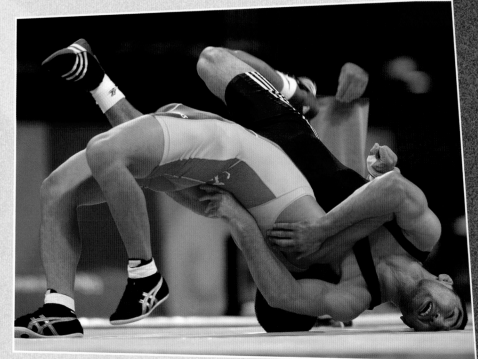

9 Half-nelson

This is a hold in which the wrestler's arm is passed under the opponent's armpit and the hand is on the back of the opponent's head. It is hard to get out of but some wrestlers manage to by turning their head away and peeling their opponent's fingers off their head.

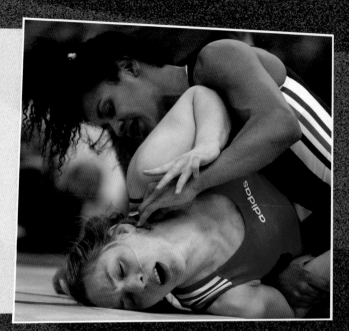

10 Cradle move

A wrestler may be firmly on her front on the mat. One way of turning her over to pin her on her back is to use a cradle move. This sees the attacker wrap one elbow behind her opponent's knee while the other arm travels around the neck. The two hands are clasped together and then the opponent is turned.

FAMOUS WRESTLERS

There have been many champion wrestlers, but to be a true legend, you have to win many championships against the very best opponents.

Amazing Aleksandr

Aleksandr Karelin of Russia was considered the best Greco-Roman wrestler. Karelin was three-time Olympic champion in the heavyweight division, and remained unbeaten for a staggering 13 years before his shock loss to American Rulon Gardner.

Karelin collected nine World Championship titles and was voted the best Greco-Roman wrestler of the twentieth century.

Unbeaten legend

At the age of just 24, Osamu Watanabe's wrestling career was over. He chose to retire straight after his brilliant gold medal for Japan at the 1964 Olympics in freestyle wrestling. During all his bouts at the Olympics, he did not give away a single point.

Osamu retired with a perfect record: 186 wins and no loses.

The Canadian champ

Canada's Christine Nordhagen-Vierling won 10 Canadian and six World Championships. In 2006, she was inducted into FILA's Hall of Fame, one of the very few female wrestlers to receive this honour.

"I've cried at the worlds every single year I've won. I've always bawled. Especially when they raise that flag and the anthem is playing. You feel so proud." – *Christine Nordhagen-Vierling*

GLOSSARY

bout
A contest between two fighters.

breakdown
The action of getting an opponent to the mat on his or her stomach or side.

bridge
The arched position a wrestler adopts to avoid his back touching the mat.

folkstyle
A style of wrestling used in US high schools and colleges, which is similar to freestyle wrestling but with some changes to rules and added safety.

freestyle
A style of wrestling in which the legs can be targeted and also used in attacks.

Greco-Roman
A style of wrestling in which the wrestler may not attack the opponent's legs nor use his own legs to perform attacks.

penetration
The action of moving forward to penetrate an opponent's defences when attacking.

pin
Forcing both of the opponent's shoulders to the mat.

professional
Professional wrestlers earn money from fighting.

self-defence
The ability to defend yourself against attack.

singlet
The one-piece uniform worn by wrestlers.

stamina
The ability to work hard for long periods.

tactics
Different ways to fight, for example defensive tactics are used to stop an opponent's attack.

throw
Any move in which a wrestler lifts the opponent from the mat then brings him back down.

FURTHER INFORMATION

BOOKS

There are many books to read about professional wrestling, but books on sports wrestling and amateur wrestling are harder to find. If you'd like to get involved in wrestling try to find a club close to where you live.

Olympic Wrestling: Great Moments in Olympic History

Barbara M. Linde (Rosen Publishing Group, 2007)
A pictorial guide to some of the great performers and bouts in Olympic history.

WWE Encyclopedia: The Definitive Guide to World Wrestling Entertainment

(Dorling Kindersely, 2009)
Lots of information on the world of WWE – the experience, the excitement – plus the history of the championship.

Greco-Roman Wrestling

William A. Martell (Human Kinetics, 1993)
Still widely available, this is one of the most thorough guides to Greco-Roman wrestling. Written by an Olympic coach, the book contains hundreds of black and white photographs.

Master This – Wrestling

Chris St John (Wayland, 2010)
Take your interest in wrestling a leap forward with this introduction, complete with step-by-step photography.

DVDs AND MOVIES

Throws and Takedowns: Freestyle Wrestling Basic / Intermediate, 2005.

Two great instructional DVDs from Geoff Thompson and available from Summersdale Productions.

Legendary (2010) – UK rating 12

A family drama about Cal Chetley, played by Devon Graye, a bright but undersized 16-year-old who joins his school's wrestling team in a bid to reunite his family, split apart by the death of his father, a college wrestling legend.

WEBSITES

http://www.fila-wrestling.com

The official website of FILA, the organisation that runs world wrestling. It features lots of news and competition results, coach's corner and much more.

http://www.britishwrestling.org

The home on the internet of the British Wrestling Association.

http://www.usawrestling.org

The official website of USA Wrestling with results, national rankings, competitions and a huge database of wrestling clubs, searchable by state.

INDEX